THE FOLLIES

THE

POEMS BY DANIEL MARK EPSTEIN

FOLLIES

THE OVERLOOK PRESS/WOODSTOCK, NEW YORK

cknowledgement is gratefully made to the following magazines in which these poems originally appeared: *The American Scholar*, *Confrontation*, and *Shenandoah*.

First published by
The Overlook Press, Inc.,
Woodstock, New York, 1977
Published in paperback in 1979 by
The Overlook Press
Lewis Hollow Road
Woodstock, N.Y. 12498

The Library of Congress Cataloged the First Printing of This Title as Follows:

PS3555
.P65F6 **Epstein, Daniel Mark.**
The Follies: poems/by Daniel Mark Epstein.— Woodstock. N.Y.: Overlook Press, 1977

48 p.; 23 cm.
ISBN 0-87951-048-X: $6.95
ISBN 0-87951-075-7 pbk. $3.45

I. Title
PS3555.P65F6 811'.5'4 76-8059
MARC

Library of Congress 78

IN MEMORIAM
ROBERT AND HENRY EPSTEIN

ONTENTS

THE FOLLIES

DUTCH

CASH ONLY, NO REFUND, NO RETURN

THE MAN WITHOUT LEGS

AT THE MILLINERY SHOP

MADEMOISELLE MALO

MIDTOWN HOME

JUDGE WINGATE'S LAMENT

JOCKEY

BERTHA

NOCTURNE

RODEMPKIN

THE FOLLIES

Blind Mr. Klugel loves the baritone of Mr. Cantini.

Mr. Klugel rocks on the back porch, listening
while his wife begins her nightly striptease
        in the bright showcase of her bedroom window:
a benefit for the ragged voyeurs of the South City
    who can look but cannot touch.

Time for all good children to be in bed.

From the tar roof of a row house over the wharves
    pours the wide baritone of the moderately drunk Mr. Cantini
singing the sun into a new country, singing
the boats to sleep in their slips, taming the oil rainbows
        to a flat shimmer in the harbor lights,
calling the stevedores to battle in dockside bars and blank alleys,
tuning up the full moon chorus of neighborhood dogs,
        summoning the sluggard moon,
waking up everybody's children.

DUTCH

Dutch in the wire cage, burning away with electrified stylus,
        or working the dye in slow along the pinpricks,
a handful of flesh at a time. High musk
of burnt flesh like the back street meat markets.
        He is some kind of artist.

My mother thought otherwise, jerking coke at the bar,
        six months out of the flatlands
she married into this garden of earthly delights:
        the ninth street shooting gallery, peep show carnival
and Dutch the tatooist,
a living advertisement of his own genius
                and the skill of his masters,
not a square foot of unadorned flesh on his whole body.

She would lead the drunk boys out by the elbow,
        whispering "this is no way to prove yourself a man,"
recalling her uncle Mack raving drunk
        clawing at vein-blue snakes drawn up his arms,
or a tale her sailor father told
                of a Swedish boy shy of the needle,
who dreamed his fear out loud
                and woke tangled in the ship's hammock,
twisted in a nightmare and the crew knew it.

And how they pitched in to get the young Swede drunk
and strapped him to the mess table
and hired a French tatooist
aboard with his packet of needles and rare dyes.
He worked a great clipper ship on the boy's chest
with full rigging
where wind would catch full in the sails when the blood cleared.

My mother would lead them away from the wire cage
while her father-in-law shouted to his son from the cash register:
"You bring a *shiksa* into a place of business . . ."
and mother:
"What kind of a Jew grows rich
from writing on a man's body?
Your laws cry out against it."
And the old man again:
"We are not Gods to make our laws for other men."

I write on your clean skin, my people,
and then dream the world will see you as you were made.

CASH ONLY, NO REFUND, NO RETURN

Earl stood on two legs when he had one to spare,
then on one leg when the cancer got him,
a short leg and a wicked crutch.
By his own count Earl was accomplice to thirty-four
murders, ninety-two muggings and five suicides.
His finger followed the headlines in the paper
spread out on a glass case that bristled with knives:
Florentine daggers, Arkansas toothpicks,
black bone and pearl-handled stilettos with blades
that kick loose and lock fast with a flick of the wrist,
Turkish daggers with serpentine blades
to snake the guts from the meanest vendetta.

He stood there in the back end of the arcade
and they came to him
from bars, the precinct lock-up, from flop-houses,
whore houses, foreclosed houses, faithless wives,
good friends gone bad, betrayals, threats, divorces.
Earl had the voice and nose of Jimmie Durante
and knew how to sell knives.
He just stood there behind the display case.

THE MAN WITHOUT LEGS

The man without legs has huge arms.
He rolls himself along Park Avenue on a skate-board,
pawing the concrete with rubber knuckles.
Sparks fly from the steel wheels of his skates.
The man without legs is the quietest beggar in the city
and makes $225.00 a week after expenses.
He looks straight ahead.
He knows pity from the inside out.

AT THE MILLINERY SHOP

She wants what no clerk in the city can bring her,
a hat that will make up her mind.
White satin speaks to the red in her cheeks,
red satin to the white.
Blue crepe shades the clear well of her eye.

She wants a hat to fit her head like an idea
so perfect only she could have dreamed it up,
a hat that draws attention to itself by disappearing
and to the head by building on it
a profusion of silent worlds in incomparable colors.

She wants a hat that can think for itself,
that will select the proper head for its household.
She turns her back on the round table-mirror
and a garden of hats on spindles,
admiring the beige lid with a feathery band.

Holding it at arm's length,
her eyes half-closed,
she leans back
under a straw bonnet crowned with flowers
that casually tries itself on her.

MADEMOISELLE MALO

Pointed ears emerge but head first
from the voluminous cloak of Mademoiselle Malo.
Her small hands lie in the black lap folds
like sleeping quail. Butter would not melt
in her mouth, but she should know better
than to allow her thoughts to run so far, unchaperoned,
from the lighthouse of her mind.

Chrysanthemums flock to the space around her head
on holiday, and in her head for all we know.
No comment, says the placard on the door
of her face, no comment.
And that's how a rumor starts, mystery tunneling

like willow roots, greater than trees.
She has turned her best face from us
and is long gone, her laughing mouth,
eyes of the stormless Atlantic under one star,
in silent discourse with an inward companion,
some prodigy of love, a small portable god.

The flowers clamor for attention, plead and scold.
Virgin white, sienna, tarnished brass,
campaign for the analytic resurrection
of Mademoiselle Malo, a young lady of parts.

MIDTOWN HOME

Snow falls so rarely nowadays and in the city
you miss that sudden whiteness of things.
So when it started in the afternoon I was on the phone
every half hour, arguing with the weather girl
and by dusk there was a good white layer on the streets
and rooftops so that in the blue twilight
the city didn't look so much like the city.

And you need it that way sometimes, especially
in January. I went out into it
and down the corridor of alleys to the park
to watch the conservatory students
slide down the walks and into the dry fountain.
The green bronze nymph was doing that backbend contortion
in a coat of snow, the same way she does it

stark naked in springtime, and with leaves
on her breasts and forehead in autumn. The bronze
war heros were reserved. But I'm sure
they must love the weather as much as I do,
and wonder why it snows so rarely these days.
I wasn't in such a hurry to get home, with night ahead,
blue light turning to red and then yellow

city light made brighter by the snow,
and I was looking in one back window and then another
        all along the brick walls of the alley.
There was this square building with green shades in the windows
                making tall white frames of light.
And I saw through a crack the sheets and rails of beds,
but nothing in them, looked like maybe

            a hospital supply house? I went closer and there
      on the nearest bed just under the window
was half a man's leg and a toothless mouth above it.
And his was only the beginning
                of a row of mouths in shrunken heads,
skins stretched thin and shining over sharp bones,
and limbs and the odds and ends of limbs, like

an ancient tribe disjointed in a higher world
                had spilled into the beds of this crowded home.
I stood trembling in pride and a deeper shame
that with all their futile suffering, borrowed breath,
I held more life in my body than they shared
              in that littered room.
They had no business being alive on a night like that.

JUDGE WINGATE'S LAMENT

Nine killers I sent to the chair, in my youth, nine
pennies in the fusebox of the law.
One willed me his wooden leg before he sat down
and prayed that I would need it before long.
God save a judge from makeshift religions of the damned.
I am weary of curses and executions.

JOCKEY

After the fourth race at Laurel.

Money talks, but Jack your twenty bucks
        won't make my horses talk.
You take me for another two-bit tout
who haunts the stables shifty-eyed
looking for high-priced nags that run outclassed?
I'll drink with you, but keep that roll in your pants.
Read the scratch sheets
and play some handicapper's tip.
                                        Or if you've got the heart
blow the whole wad on a long shot and be done.

Straight Bourbon. You are a gentleman.
You look me in the eye. And yet you see this
hump that bends my body like an overloaded branch:
it didn't come from pitching hay
or shoveling shit from the paddock to the barn.
This back-pack started as a jockey's crouch
        to hide from the wind that fights your stride.
I was light but held my horse's sides
                                        between my legs like a vise,
broke fast and rode hard for the rails,
had my share of the winners but loved them all.
I was the horse's mind, he was my heart.

Then I rode a doctored bay at Pimlico
                    some millionaire had high-nerved for a race,
deadened her leg so she'd run free of the pain.
Well she ran like a champ until the foreleg snapped
in the backstretch with the grandstand thundering, I went down
under the hooves of those nags she'd left behind.
One beat my shoulder like a gob of dough
                                        and it began to rise.

So the stable was through with me,
the horse-faced women who take the jockey to bed
                                        for a tip and a hard ride,
and tall jades who long to mother a boy-sized man.

Yet I rode for love of the horses, maybe
I'm worth more to them from the ground
than I ever was from their backs.
You know you're betting on a field of cripples
                         that should be scratched and set to graze?
Look how that roan bolts and halts when he's walked:
                    he's run his race in the paddock.

That grey has grown boxing-glove ankles.
I've had him stand
all afternoon in a tub of ice to shrink them down.
Another horse runs so doped with azium
                                        he'll run in a dream
and win or lose in a dream.

So you take me for a hunchback fool
because I still won't take you for your money.
          Well then lay it on the line.
The measure of a man is the speed
               his dream races through the world. You bet
dead money because your life isn't gamble enough.
                                    See that chestnut mare in the ring—
no daisycutter, she has a great heart to ride;
when she gallops it's a song and you feel
                         steel springs under you, standing at the rail.
I rode her mother fifteen years ago,
                                   a bright bay dream of sixteen hands,
Cloudland by Wrack out of Fairy Ray by Radium.

BERTHA

A local brewery was charged with negligence in an alleged chimney fire. Defense lawyers argued that the flue was so constructed and maintained, that it *could not* catch fire. One witness for the defense, a chimney sweep, set forth his evidence in the following terms:

That there man as saw two yards of flame coming out of her
 never seen no such thing I say.
No soot or coal ever sticks in her throat
 to catch fire, the wind won't let it stop:
there's wind in her would blow you out like a feather
 if you didn't know her well.
There ain't a brick in her doesn't know my foot.
I go all around the boiler then
I twist in the chimney like smoke and then
 up I goes with the wind.
Your honor I was brought up in that chimney
and I'll be sworn the sides of her is as clean
 this minute as I am.

NOCTURNE

1

Moonlight, sly weaver and loom of my sunflower,
darkness has found you out,
midnight and the night-vision of lovers.
I am on the street in the greater darkness of man-made light,
a watchman working the graveyard shift.
I'm a safe-cracker tunneling underground dreams,
a second-story man
flying owl-wise on a draft of nightmares.
You were burning the midnight oil, my pale conspirator,
and got caught in the act.

By night and the powers of darkness
I am making a day to live in.
I will gather a dawn from this running starlight.
From glittering eyes of street women, gambler's sweat
and the final tears of a kidnapped boy in an alley
I will stitch a fine dew for my lawn.
Sunflowers shall be the light of my garden,
woven in secrecy, the moon's genius.

2

Grand and eternal creator! Hand
        that spun out the fine rage of the hummingbird,
eye that winked the ox-eye daisy into bloom, you
who pitch the sky tent and drive golden pegs at the horizon—
if I haven't time enough for you in this world
        it's not that I don't care.
My beloved creator, you have not lived in my house.
The one I'm building isn't finished yet.
There are few enough signs of you in the room that I rent.
So, with humility, I am taking
                certain matters of creation into my feeble hands.

How shall I make my city?
I shall build with granite stones and blocks of mud,
I shall frame with a plank of oak and a beaverboard,
                windowless walls and windows without walls.
I shall nail with galvanized steel and rusted iron.
I shall build the square shells for snails
        and monuments to Federalist pride and Victorian fear.
I shall let the strong stand
                and topple weak structure with my wrecking balls.

3

I am building a song to live in
                and how shall I make my people?
There will be men of iron and men of tin,
            women of brick and women of blue slate,
people of clay and people of straw,
                        wooden ornament and gold.
I shall make my people the same substance as their dwellings
                and the spirit of their songs.

No man or woman shall hold public office
            who is not in the grace of God and the nine muses,
who cannot sing and pray.
No man shall sweep the streets with the great-wheeled carts
who does not love a clean street and the song of the great wheel.
No woman shall bring a child into the world
                        who does not know the song of creation.

What am I bid for my handiwork, my white elephant?

Who am I kidding?
I'm the luckiest man in the world
if I can give it away.
I see one taker:
Lady, you promised me more than a mortal can pay.
You, woman, you know who I'm talking to.

I have given you jade trinkets and opal rings,
the second for bad luck, the first for good.
If I am the source of all riches, don't take advantage.
If I am the final source of evil,
take back this talisman you gave me
in a time of true sympathy for my innocent fear.

4

Moonlight, sly weaver and loom of my sunflower,
                    all that is good in me loves darkness,
all that is evil loves the light.
If I have not given the truth then tell me
what is the truth, and if I have not made good
my promises, then what have I done?

            I have driven a thousand miles after her
                    and I have left her alone.

I have loved three women well and some dozen
        better than we deserved.
Now I'd give the whole storm of them and their long memories
      for one who would hold me
through this single night.

RODEMPKIN

THE EXCURSION

Rodempkin was custodian of two griefs
and a mixed blessing:
a friend in hell and a wife in heaven on his account,
and a bawling scourge on earth
that was his only company and kin.
The boy was willed to Rodempkin by his wife
and by God who rewarded the mother's trial with heaven.

Rodempkin took the death of his good wife
as mortification short of holy penance, a crime
to punish a crime and double his mortal sin;
for he'd sent his best friend to hell from a poker game.
Duncan was no believer
and when the cards ran too long in Rodempkin's favor
Duncan pointed a long jack-knife at Rodempkin
who grabbed a tire-iron off the gashouse wall
and rang a dull death knell on Duncan's skull.

Witnesses swore he'd swung in self-defense.
A jury found Rodempkin innocent
and yet he brooded on this crime.
When his dear wife died he wouldn't borrow
his wife's blood to pay for Duncan's,
but loaded guilt on a groaning conscience in his sorrow.

He quit his job and took to a strict diet of saltless cabbage
        that made a sulphurous rumbling in his bowels;
he wore his clothes until they stood alone.
He took to reading Aquinas and counting his sins
        like sheep until a fitful sleep would take him
away into dreams where his victims were alive
            and no one could wake him.

Formula bottles exploded on the stove.
Rodempkin forgot them, but the baby wouldn't.
Social workers finally answered the child's alarms
                        relieving Rodempkin of maternal duty.

Rodempkin had two passions (besides remorse):
one was theology, the practical science of religion, the other—
science, the practical religion, specifically electron physics.
Knowing the first would lead to self-chastisement
            he put aside Aquinas, Buber, Tillich and Plotinus
and built a laboratory in his garage
full of tunnel diode amplifiers and cloud chambers
and other instruments of torture and delight:
tuned collector oscillators that catch the current
                        and whirl it around in a flywheel polka,
step up and step down power transformers
            that turn water drops of energy into a flood,
then weary the flood and dry it to a trickle.

The tar roof bristled with antennae,
micro-wave and horn reflectors and radar.
And Rodempkin delighted in the push-pull
of amplifiers designed to tune
the howling sine-wave music of the spheres
in circuits of series and parallel resonance.
With peaked and sawtoothed waves of commanded frequency
he'd caress and pluck the strings of energy
until circuits hummed and yodeled in divine harmony
to shame Orpheus and make a deaf cripple dance.

Rodempkin studied Maxwell and Ben Franklin,
Faraday, Buck Fuller and Democritus.
He learned enough of theory to confuse him
and in his confusion believe he knew the truth.
His walls were decorated with schematics
like hieroglyphs on the walls of a savage temple.
He built broadcasters and receivers
to call Bangkok and regale Alaska
and with his spirit cavorting on short-waves,
found sporadic respite from his guilt.
And then his mind would wander.

One twilight he tinkered innocently with a tuner
and was seduced by the glow of a diode tube.

Twilight hour, when fever rages in mind and body,
gazing on the glowing gold space charge
between cathode and anode, Rodempkin was trapped.
His vision entered first into the vacuum, then the mercurial soul
of Rodempkin plunged into the current that flowed
from fiery tungsten filament to dark anode,
dodging electrons boiling off the crimson rod.

What a view from here!
With an opposite charge on either hand:
one positive and bright
one negative and dark,
Rodempkin meditated, like a manichean on a mountaintop
or an eyelidless Buddhist master in his cave.
He surveyed unadorned forces of darkness and light,
love and strife, and good and evil.
Intrepid explorer Rodempkin rubbed his eyes and saw
heaven and hell, the dominions of every atom!
"Electrons are the source of all our troubles,
every one a mischievous devil
in the marrow atoms of our bones and souls.
Proton and neutron of the nucleus,
these are a stalwart heaven,
stable and integral and virtuous,
while the dark electron like a wandering moon
leads men on to madness and to hell."

In the midst of these reveries a woman's face
rose out of the hypnotic cathode charge,
the haloed face of Rodempkin's martyred wife.
He would have poured his remorse into the void,
but she turned to fire as swiftly as she'd come.
And in the shadow of the electrode he saw
the silouette of Duncan carved out of the darkness,
lips twisted, jaw set against eternal pain.

"Let bygones be bygones Duncan," he began,
but Duncan faded and he was alone.
"If they won't stay to hear me out I'll go to them,"
he cried, "or I'll go mad."

But he was mad already. His beard
grew shadows on his jaw, his clothing
absorbed his atrabilious humors
so that dogs wouldn't go near him.
So Rodempkin was protected from the world
to pursue his arcane studies and designs.
Researching laws of electro-magnetism
he learned magnetic fields form around a current
like armies around a martial head of state.

And as armies surround and order their general
and make him more resolute
so the magnetic field
polarizes any matter that lies within it.
Thus the mysterious loadstone
grown wise from sleeping in the earth,
leads men home on land and sea.

"And why not make a magnet of myself?
The world for a worldly soul is simply *ground*,
where all charges are harum-scarum, neutralized.
But look at the saint, the halo round his head
glows like the space charge in electron tubes.
His head must be in heaven.
I'll ring heaven in a halo around my head
long enough to finish my business in paradise
and then grow horns to make my way through hell.
No, first I'll send the electrons to my head
and see if the devil doesn't claim my soul.
And when the charge wears off and my soul returns,
I'll reverse the field and send the protons to my brain,
fold my hands and pray to meet my maker."

RODEMPKIN IN HELL

So Rodempkin built a monstrous induction coil
like a huge tension spring or a spiraling snake
whose mouth struck at one wall of the garage
and tail stretched tickling the other.
And he suspended a narrow pallet within the coil
where he could lie down,
then hooked each end of the coil to a power supply
that drove enough voltage to light up half the town.
Rodempkin lay trembling within the coil, uncertain
whether bound for heaven or for hell,
and pulled a switch at his hip.
There was a horrendous buzzing
as if a swarm of bees had stormed the garage,
smoke billowed from the transformers and white sparks flew.
He lay entranced. The blood gone to his head
convinced Rodempkin he was polarized.
The dark energy of his past rushed up through his frame,
black deeds of his youth called one by one to mind,
tortured cats, forged I.D.'s and murders,
an army of evil that made camp on his brow.

Rodempkin shuddered and crawled out of the coil.
He kicked open the garage door
and drew deep in his lungs a draught of rush hour air.
"So this is hell," he muttered, and set out
toward the city, like a sleepwalker searching a dream
for a watch or a golden thought lost in the daylight,
whose mind explores and paints the darkness in its image,
a world where the lost treasure is sure to be found.
Rodempkin wandered through stalled traffic
where cars stood bumper to bumper and hubcap to cap,
the drivers howling away their twilight hour.
Threading the traffic afoot Rodempkin reached
the toll bridge to the heart of hell.

Without a car he couldn't enter.
So he scrambled down the mud bank and gazed on the river,
picking his way amid shards, tin cans and detergent foam.
"This is the river Acheron. I see it burning
far off, black as oil, and the whirlpools churning.
I'll wait here for Charon the gondolier."

A clatter under bridge girders and lusty singing
a secular and profane air
about a lady of easy virtue from Princess Anne:
it was a ragged grizzled randy bum
armed with a gallon of reeking Gallo Ripple
from which he gulped long drafts between choruses
to warm his bowels and ease the passage of his song.
He waved the bottle cheerfully at Rodempkin, who
came skulking toward him. "I'm not one of the damned,"
he said. "No more than any of us," replied the bum.
"Sit down and have a drink, looks like you need it."
"I want to cross the river Acheron
into Hell. Salvation is half mine
if one soul damned in hell will forgive me."

Now greed and compassion fought for the upper hand
to pick Rodempkin's pocket or proffer aid.
There's not one sot on earth who doesn't know
the pathos of that single word, *forgive*,
or a panhandler who can't tell a mark from another bum.
Stumbling under the bridge, this bum dragged out
a trough crusted with grey cement, and a scantling plank
down to the water and waved Rodempkin aboard.
"For ten bucks I'll pole you over."

So the world's currency holds good in the underworld,
        mused Rodempkin as he paid and boarded.
Good news for trade, a new foreign market for exchange.
The bum sang for joy as he dug his pole into the mud,
        for his conscience had drawn a truce
with Armageddon. An angel and demon powered his craft.

Rodempkin disembarked on a dusty garden
        park where trees only grew to spite the ground.
Nettles thrived and ravenous weeds, flowers died in the stem.
Pigeons hatched in grime clung to twisted branches,
        their vile plumage groomed by the poison air,
and squawked as if too ugly to coo or sing.

There he met a white haired evangelist
        who buttonholed him chanting "there's still time—
put aside thine evil ways and walk with God."
Rodempkin looked on the lost soul pityingly.
"Sad wretch, you prove a man's life destines his hell.
You are messiah in a long foredamned Judea
        condemned to strive
against The Dark in the dark, on its home ground.
What earthly crime demands such retribution, did you
        rape children, or disembowel a saint?"

"I was lost in darkness but Christ has lighted my path.
I am bathed in glory."
This outburst questioned hell's efficiency:
true hell for a messianic sinner
would surely be a convent or monastery
where piety graces every breath and gesture.
In hell he is in his glory, a Napoleon of the cross
with heathen worlds to conquer.
Perhaps this is a harpy, thought Rodempkin, one of the happy
citizens of hell for whom it's paradise.
Isn't one man's torment another's heaven?
Could be he's on a cultural exchange
to enrich his ecstasy and their desolation.

"Citizen or fellow traveler, can you tell me the way
to the innermost circle of the underworld?"
The evangelist pointed solemnly to the Block
where tempestuous citizens take their pleasure,
where flesh is bought and sold, salted and pickled
with alchohol and other drugs that lift the spirits
only to hurl them crashing down again.

A thousand women in the shape of sin,
dacron-laced and painted, electric haired,

a thousand leering mouths in hanging flesh.
Gay boys who walk an empty street
obliquely, as if shouldering through a crowd,
boys who eat men
and laugh with the women.
Cheap rifle crack of the shooting gallery cowboy
and the barker's shout that can lure and deafen.
Old world with a worn heart
only fit for wrecks with long memories.
"So the torment of the wicked is
to persist in their idle wickedness."
Rodempkin strode among familiar buildings where laughter rang,
bottles clinked and glasses shattered, the juke-box
grumbled under its base load.
"Eternal castigation of the flesh, the fire
that burns but will not consume—"
He waved aside the greasy hands of whores,
swung open the door to a second story poolhall
where he'd played, before God and misfortune had clouded his brain.

Rodempkin entered the smoking triangular light
and caught the jaded eye of a ship-fitter, an old crony,
a short and spiteful man
who collared the ragged Rodempkin and drew him close,
then sniffed and pushed him away.

"Boys, God damn if it ain't that saint Rodempkin
                    come here to shoot pool or sing us all a hymn.
How's that wife of yours, as good a lay as ever?"
                                        "Dead and gone to a better place than this,"
he answered. And the company dropped their cues
                    and set upon Rodempkin, for this was hell
and cruelty the national pastime.

They told lurid stories of his wife, how good
                the silken stroke of her fingers, her quick snatch;
they asked about Duncan and Rodempkin broke
                        from their blue-chalked hands, stumbling
to a long back table where a stranger
shot straight pool alone.
Although the man was as strange to Rodempkin as Buddha,
Redempkin fell before him on his knees
                        begging forgiveness and calling Duncan's name,
and smothered his hand with kisses of true repentence.

Restless souls want carnivals. What could be better
    sport than the suffering of a fellow creature?
The side-show freak we cage or harness in a stall,
        the lion-faced lady, the man with a third eye,
the man with a twin growing out of his side like a human bat,

the man with a monstrous grief, these are all game
where the prize is rare pleasure for every player
but the victim. We lock our agonies with the beast
in his cage, the bound victim sets us free
from the pain love would exact in greater measure.
Cruelty is the backhand of a caress,
celebration of divorce
between estranged components of the soul.
While love hides in the palm, the fist protects
the frail passion that might kill itself through kindness.

Dress Rodempkin in a motley coat, scramble his brains
and tie a tin can to his tail.
Fuel your virile laughter with his tears.
Fill a pool table with hundreds of billiard balls,
make him walk up and down them singing
Ave Maria and Mea Culpa.
And when his feet lose their grip and fly,
beat him back into line with a pool cue
or bottle, or whatall is at hand,
till he reaches the far end where the stranger stands,
Rodempkin's Frankenstein of human compassion.
He commands Rodempkin to his battered knees
and whacks him about the shoulders with the cue
by way of chivalrous ceremony.
Pronounces the pilgrim forgiven, and clubs him again.
Rodempkin swoons away in ecstasy.

RODEMPKIN IN HEAVEN

"I am half penanced" said Rodempkin, "yet
I am not fit for heaven. I must shave
and bathe my body in rosewater and buy a suit
and play the part of a man who nears the grave."
Rodempkin perfected his toilet,
lay reversed in the afterlife machine, and looked above
the mean trappings of this world, like a city preacher
with an eye for God and love for every creature.
Where heaven before had lain at his feet,
he now kicked hell, with his head in paradise.
He flipped the switch, the dynamos coughed and sputtered,
fuses blew again, likewise
Rodempkin's hold on the world, like a buttered
marble. "Matilda," he cried,
"I am cast like a skiff unruddered
into a gloomy heaven, a blind bird in the sky.
Have mercy on me and lead me within your sight
so I might hear your sweet forgiveness this night."

Rodempkin crawled out of the coil,
this time a blessed man.
He felt the glow of the nimbus around his ears
and lightness afoot, as if invisible wings
had rooted in his shoulder blades to whisk him along.

His soul was as light as the white of a dove's wing
except for the blemish a woman's word could brush away.
Rodempkin took the same road to the City of God
he had taken to hell, but he didn't know it,
the world and the road so changed with his change of clothes.
Angels smiled on him from every side as he glided
through Elysian Fields where glorious fountains
of lawn sprinklers saluted the sun with high rainbows
and each polished car was a chariot for the new-born.
Rush hour was past, the bridge traffic was light,
and Rodempkin cat-walked the girders with such aplomb
no one could stop him.

So he went autoless on the guardrail over Jordan,
up to the golden gate built by the Chamber of Commerce,
endorsed by all the city's saints and archangels.
He hung around the gates waiting for Saint Peter
and the bum that had played Charon ambled by,
picking up a cigar butt at Rodempkin's feet.
Rodempkin's body was transfigured beyond recognition,
and his mind transfigured beyond recognizing
the bum: "This must be Peter," judged Rodempkin,
"dressed like the humble fisherman."

"Can you spare a quarter for a man down on his luck?"
        Rodempkin took this as a test
of good will and charity, and dug in his pocket,
        surprised to find his cash transubstantiated
with his flesh, and with current value even in heaven.
The bum's eyes glowed as Rodempkin peeled a five
        from his crumpled roll, and the bum danced
and kicked his heels and sang out "God will reward you!"
which Rodempkin took for a visa to God's throne.

Tell Muse, if you can spare an hour
            from herding the poets that wander this hemisphere
bleating out more verses than there are ears to hear them
or reasons, and books that booksellers drive from field to market
            that never would be noticed but for their numbers.
Tell what Rodempkin saw in heaven.
For I have no Beatrice to guide me there,
      nor Dante's vision, my eyes are weak
like the slits of a kitten's eyes with birth mist still in them.
My world is a half millenium farther away
              from heaven than it was in Dante's time,
and time is a feeble gauge of the true distance
            year has begotten of year since the last dance
of our innocent ancestors in the garden.
Tell us what there was on earth
              for the mad Rodempkin to anamorphose into heaven.

First he saw a marching regimental band and choir,
not the martial force that subdues souls
with bomb and cannon, rather
the sort that brings you to your knees with kindness and good will.
Decked out in black parade gear, red epaulets,
an army of salvation that sells
hot coffee and toast in hostels for a prayer
to tramps whose apostasy can't hold a candle to their hunger.
Rodempkin heard these as a choir of angels. He fell in
and followed them with borrowed tambourin
to Lexington market where Rodempkin's appetite
revived with all the ardor of his soul. He hadn't eaten in a day
and heaven, like the best resort hotels
must proscribe hunger past a dwindled satiety.

There is every food a man could wish for in the market
and some he couldn't until he saw them there.
Raw, cooked and half-cooked, charbroiled, baked and fried—
many a hungry visitor there
has sworn he must have died and gone to heaven.
Piled on ice, the goggle-eyed gaping trout,
rockfish with black cross-hatching and sea bass
whose grey-green scales gleam like a storm-tossed ocean,
speckled mullet, the iron-backed oyster, who
like a tight-thighed woman opens hard
to reveal the silken-skinned pearl.

What does the fat butcher stand smiling guard over
with bloodied apron and his murderous cleaver?
A hill of pink capons and fresh stewers,
chicken thighs and legs and breasts and turkey necks.
Fowls who cry loud in the killing make good eating.
The lamb old enough to bleed is old enough to butcher.
Red skeins of ground round, short ribs and the black jelly
of baby calves liver,
just think of that black jelly slowly sliced
with razor-sharp naked steel,
finger thick, and fried with onions! It'll take
the place of whatever liver you drank away
last night. Continents of porterhouse steak for the rich
and pig-foot, ham-hock, slab bacon and pork brain
for those whose money jingles.

Me, I've never been able to separate
the vendors from their wares.
The buxom piece who carves the veal is more a bargain
than all the filet mignon of seven markets
set out for the taking at half-price.
The blue-eyed angel juggling vegetables, the touch
of her long fingers on my tomatoes is worth the cost
of five pyramids of pomegranites and Spanish melon!

Rodempkin ordered a fried chicken wing and wandered munching
                through this world-spawned cornucopeia of heaven,
the proudest trumpet of the modern tribe, in whose mouth
men stand hip to haunch in holiest communion.

And still there are holy wars. In an empty stall
three cops with night sticks pommeled lean ribs of a boy
swearing bitterly they'd teach him how to steal.
"Well, the guardians of justice must have their heaven
and what paradise for cops
would lack such specimens for corporal torture.
Likely this boy is marred with original sin,
reinforced by a life of dissipation
and on loan from hell to enrich their eternal home."
At this thought Rodempkin dropped his chicken bone
                and ran from the market, down the street
and stopped at the first man who seemed to have the time
for him, a lecher with his fly down
    leaning in an alley, whistling to the girls.

Why did Rodempkin always find
                        himself in colloquy with idlers,
prophets, rogues and peripatetic crackpots?
            Nobody's more generous than a bum
who's lost so much and has so little to give.

These are the salt of the earth, the philanthropists,
worn-heeled, motheaten, the true Samaritans.
The man that's gone flat broke and down on his luck,
the man whose thought has jumped the track,
has all the time in the world for his kind.
This is why whole armies of woe-bedraggled tramps
are maintained on city streets,
for local color, and for fellowship.
You call them dregs of the culture, derelicts.
Yet they're walking insurance
you won't be there unattended,
sir and madam, when *you* fall.

Rodempkin's wife never went second class,
so he asked the lecher the way to the seventh heaven.
"If you got the cash there ain't
a house in town can work you over like Aunt Lil's.
Around the World, Sixty-nines, French Pool and Fell's Point Tickle,
they'll bathe your hide in honey-oil and lick you dry,
they'll swallow your balls and hum a lullabye
till every hair on your body stands on end
vibrating like a light gauge banjo string.
There are women every color, shape and size
and age, from thirteen to sixty-five
(retirement age for whores as well as teachers.

If she hasn't married the mayor by then she'll be
slinging chow mein in a bust-out chinese joint—
        they also serve who only stand and wait)
black, blond, creme de cao cao and octaroon,
women as big as two, two the size of one,
women with beards and moustaches (a kiss without whiskers
        is like an egg without salt) for men
who have no whiskers of their own.
Women with silicone breasts like marble stones
                that look fine from ten feet but careful not
to roll over on them unpadded, they're pitiless
        and apt to pop if bitten . . ."

Lil's "Seventh Heaven Hotel"
                was on the Block where Rodempkin had found hell.
Red neon blazoned the name above the door
        THE SEVENTH HEAVEN—VACANCIES.
Although every room was occupied, the lobby crammed
            at every hour of the day or night,
the turnover was fantastic, so a bed
was always emptied in an hour or two,
            or half a bed, which suits a sleepless man.
Nor did the service drive the guests away
        who'd pay a night's rent any hour of the day.
It was a normal hotel except for the traffic
    and the mysterious angle of the stairs
that seemed much easier to climb than to descend,
                    the way strong men flew up them and stumbled down.

Lil was chief room clerk, a solid matron,
    a pillar of decadent respectability
who had reached her position
(from lying to standing) by grim frugality.
A woman of unaccountable age, her face applied in layers
    of paint and plaster like the hotel walls,
that flaked and peeling told of eroded glory.
    Her breasts she rested on the countertop
        to keep them from the floor.
A pearl-handled pistol on her hip she wore
to speak when a woman's voice could not be heard.

"Is my Matilda here?" Rodempkin asked this formidable dame,
who fingered the keys that jingled on a chain
around her neck. "You want Matilda? Christ,
I thought no one would ever ask.
She's been off her feed for weeks.
I was about to put her business on the street.
Number twelve, and pay up in advance—"

Rodempkin traded ten dollars for the key
    and mounted the stairs slowly, so slowly
the waiting customers stood amazed.
Rodempkin was like a seaman washed on shore
    after three days of dreaming on the land,

a pilgrim at the end of a holy journey
whose shrine heaves into sight. He must savor
the last tremulous moment before his dream
can stand the daylight.
Never did a young girl creep home late
and tread the hall by her parents door so softly
as Rodempkin tiptoed down this corridor.
On either side he could hear the lovers pant and moan,
seraphs stroking through a blissful lake.
Never did a youth at his girl friend's door
fit a key, turn a lock so deftly as Rodempkin
opening this sanctum sanctorum, an angel's prison.

The whore lay on the bed face down where she had fallen
top heavy from consuming half a fifth
of Southern Comfort. The bottle glowed on the vanity.
Rodempkin pulled a chair to her bedside and took her hand
so not to awaken her cruelly.
He whispered her name in her ear. She rolled,
her hand before the light, slowly revealing
a woman worthy neither a poet's praise nor a lecher's censure.
No longer young, she retained a dim flush of her youth
like a fire died down to embers that glowed through her paint.
Her hair was dulled from bleach but not yet withered,
her body showed wear but wasn't yet worn through.
She blinked and moaned, her tiny hand shaded her eyes.
And peeking through her fingers she spied Rodempkin.

This was the loveliest angel he'd ever seen,
the dream in whom salvation was invested,
his soul, and wife or not, she was a woman.
"What do you want," she groaned.
"I thought I'd gotten rid of the last of you.
I lie here like a rotten fish.
Better go knock for another chick
or work it off with your hands,"
she mumbled, voice thick with alcohol,
and rolled on her belly, glaring at the wall.

"I've come so far to hear your blessed voice
break the fever that's on my mind.
I don't ask you to forget your suffering or my crimes.
Call them to mind again and know
I have taken every lash double on my own back.
Forgive me, trade me back my innocence."
And Rodempkin spoke this sacred word "forgive"
as if his life hung with it on his lips. The whore
took stock and sobered, rolled over and sat up.
She heard Rodempkin's story from first to last.
Rodempkin, lunatic, poet and lover combined
made such music of his journey that her love
coiled round his mad song like a serpent charmed by a flute.

"You want me to forgive you," she pouted.
"In ten years of turning tricks this is the queerest.
Here I lay mourning over my damned soul and a shot life,
        a cheap tart's wardrobe and no man but a pimp,
wondering what kind of a God would give me time
to hear my sins. They'd fill a book you couldn't lift.
            And what have you done?"
"I've murdered you."
                        "You bet you have, you
and a thousand like you who pay my rent."

Then Rodempkin wept, the whore broke down as well,
        oh there was a great chorus of weeping in Seventh Heaven.
She promised to forgive him if he'd make
            an honest woman of her,
take her out of the Seventh Heaven and make her a wife.
"But my dear, we're already married," protested Rodempkin.
            "That was on earth and in another life.
                    All true marriages are made in heaven."

THE WEDDING SONG

Lay down the day's business, citizens, artisans,
workers in wool and law and larceny,
put aside your mechanical looms, your courtroom briefs and lies.
Stevedores drop your cargo at the dock,
clerks of the law, dry goods and grocery,
lay down your wares.
And you, daughters of a great house, the Seventh Heaven,
leave your beds and drop your tools,
get up, there is a spectacle under way
that calls for a whole city to swear to.
Good citizens, who knows but witnessing this your tongues,
so strange to the truth, will need no other songs
but true ones to relate this miracle, this union
of an honest woman and an innocent man.
Why should she lie, whose history
is public domain, what does he know
of evil, who has sinned and been forgiven?

Sisters-in-lawlessness, wake up the bride.
She's been in bed too long, this is no time
for sleeping or dreaming. The steeples all
have bells in their throats that call and sing,
quick pigeons coo in the tin gutters,
the groom is pawning his gold watch for a ring.
Bathe the bride in the smoothest bath-oils of Arpege,
for her body is chaffed with years of hard use.

She wants her hand silk-smooth, to take the ring
    like an unskilled virgin's finger.
Sponge her with elephant ears and coconut oil.
Rinse the lacquer from her radiant hair and let it fall
        around her shoulders. Give back
to the rhythm of nature the years
that unnatural acts have painted on her face.
And let her shine in this mystical union,
        an honest woman for an innocent man.

Carry the wedding gown high on your shoulders,
      don't let it drag the ground.
This day she must be arrayed in purity,
      her dacron dress should seem
woven from spun diamonds that can't remember coal.
Make her veil transparent as her history,
                    visible only in the folds,
to protect her from light of ill fame and admit the good.
Make the veil drape her face as gracefully
        as shadows through swaying trees on a still lake.
Florests, wire down from every shop
            hot-house blossoms for her garland. Strew the path
with torrid roses and lilies with high scent
       and monstrous orchids that have never felt the pin,
carnations rescued from the buttonholes
              of strait-jacketed socialites.

And bring wild daisies who hold the blinding sun in their eyes.
For this is a match that heaven must smile upon,
                    this honest woman and this innocent man.

Whenever did mortal man deserve such treasure,
                a bride that needs no tutoring in love's dances,
no stitch of a maiden, but a full blown woman
  of whole cloth to wrap a husband in,
no spring trickle, an autumn flood to drown a man?
And when did a woman ever wed a man
                who suffered so long to find her, as this groom?
You upright guardians of the secular law, work today
policemen, neither for low graft, nor high city pay.
      Hold back the honking traffic from the Block
                so the thoroughfare
becomes a temple aisle. Dock carpenters
bring hammers and rip saws and ten-penny nails,
                build a high grandstand in front of Lil's Hotel
with scaffold and altarpiece
and a wedding arch of latticework and beams
to frame for the present view and future recall,
    this honest woman and this innocent man.